R

COLLINS

Glasgow & London

First published 1990
Copyright © William Collins Sons & Company Limited
Published by William Collins Sons & Company Limited
Printed in Hong Kong
ISBN 0 00 435784-1

HOW TO USE THIS BOOK

Your Collins Traveller Guide will help you find your way around your chosen destination quickly and easily. It is colour-coded for easy reference:

The blue-coded 'topic' section answers the question 'I would like to see or do something; where do I go and what do I see when I get there?' A simple, clear layout provides an alphabetical list of activities and events, offers you a selection of each, tells you how to get there, what it will cost, when it is open and what to expect. Each topic in the list has its own simplified map, showing the position of each item and the nearest landmark or transport access, for instant orientation. Whether your interest is Architecture or Food you can find all the information you need quickly and simply. Where major resorts within an area require in-depth treatment, they follow the main topics section in alphabetical order.

The red-coded section is a lively and informative gazetteer. In one alphabetical list you can find essential facts about the main places and cultural items - 'What is La Bastille?', 'Who was Michelangelo?' - as well as practical and invaluable travel information. It covers everything you need to know to help you enjoy yourself and get the most out of your time away, from Accommodation through Babysitters, Car Hire, Food, Health, Money, Newspapers, Taxis and Telephones to Zoos.

Cross-references: Type in small capitals - CHURCHES - tells you that more information on an item is available within the topic on churches. A-Z in bold - **A-Z** - tells you that more information is available on an item within the gazetteer. Simply look under the appropriate heading. A name in bold - **Holy Cathedral** - also tells you that more information on an item is available in the gazetteer under that particular heading.

Packed full of information and easy to use - you'll always know where you are with your Collins Traveller Guide!

Photographs by **Michael Siebert**

Helios, the sun god, fell in love with Rhodes when he saw her emerging from the waves after the great flood sent by Zeus. Mortals have been enchanted by 'the isle of the roses' ever since. The sun rules the whole island for around 300 days of the year. Spring until late Autumn is an almost unbroken chain of sunny days and warm balmy nights. Roses, hibiscus, bougainvillea, jasmine and honeysuckle flourish. The scent of Rhodes is unforgettable.

For the tourist the island can provide almost everything. Swimming in beautiful bays, or lazing on beaches of golden sand. Drinking ouzo in water-front cafes, watching the rich toy with their yachts. Exploring the maze of the Old Town of Rhodes. It's a relaxing place. There is little crime and not even a jail. Offenders have to catch the ferry to Kos, another Dodecanese island, to go to prison.

The best way to arrive is by boat, sailing between the statues of a stag and a hind on pillars at the entrance to Mandraki harbour. If you don't have your own yacht, cheat a little. Take one of the many boat trips from Mandraki and imagine the return trip is the first time you have seen the harbour - one of the most romantic in the Mediterranean.

The Colossus of Rhodes, one of the seven wonders of the world, reputedly straddled the entrance to Mandraki. Scholars now say the statue was elsewhere in the town, but the setting is so perfect you feel the story could be true. Mandraki itself, with windmills on one side, is dominated by the Old Town's honey coloured walls, originally built in the middle ages by the Knights of St John, and restored this century by occupying Italians inspired by Mussolini's dream of making the Mediterranean a Roman sea again.

Rhodes is today one of the most cosmopolitan of the Greek islands. Modern Rhodes Town can compete with many European cities in its stock of designer label goods. Strangely for an island so dominated by the sun there are also dozens of shops selling umbrellas and fur coats. The Old Town, hiding behind its thick walls, is a maze of streets and alleys. Narrow lanes between shuttered houses suddenly open up into tree-shaded squares, with tavernas and bars. The main streets, once patrolled by Crusaders, are lined with shops and stalls, selling ceramics, leather goods, paintings and souvenirs.

Take a boat to Lindos, now a whitewashed fishing village, but once the island's capital. The little town, with its sandy beach and the only natural harbour on the island, nestles under another fortress built by the Knights of St John in the Middle Ages. Above the castle on the Acropolis are the remains of a 4thC BC temple to Lindian Athena.

Visit ancient Ialyssos and Kamiros which, with Lindos pre-date the founding of Rhodes Town. Ialyssos has an underground shrine to St George with beautifully restored frescoes depicting the life of Christ. Christianity mingles with earlier religions. There are remains of a Doric fountain and a temple to Athena and Zeus. Kamiros was abandoned at the time of Christ after about five centuries of decline. The ruins of the ancient buildings have been excavated. Tourist guides will tell you it's the Rhodian equivalent of Pompeii.

Walk through Petaloudes, the valley of the butterflies, and marvel at them in their thousands, apparently asleep on the trunks of trees. Visitors are asked to go quietly and not to disturb them.

Since Helios began his affair with the island there have been other suitors - and most were rough. For 5000 years waves of invaders occupied the island. Among them were the Minoans from Crete who colonised the island and built shrines for moon worship. Warriors from Rhodes fought at Troy. In 305 BC Demetrius the Besieger, King of Macedonia, spent almost a year trying to take the island's capital. He built a huge siege tower ten storeys high, with built-in grappling hooks and catapults. When the siege failed the defenders sold the siege engine and used the cash to pay for a massive statue of the sun god. Completed by Charles of Lindos in about 290 BC the Colossus stood for 65 years until an earthquake caused it to buckle at the knees and fall. Tradition has it that the statue lay where it had fallen until the mid-17thC AD when Arab raiders carried the bronze off and sold it for scrap in Syria. Romans, Goths, Persians and Arabs all attacked the island in the centuries that followed. Eventually Rhodes was occupied by Genoese pirates from whom the Knights of St John, in retreat from the Holy Land, bought the island. By the early part of the 14thC the Crusaders had begun their impressive fortifications. For more than 200 years they held the island against frequent attack until they finally surrendered, after a 145-day siege, to Sultan Suleiman the Magnificent and left for Malta. Four hundred relatively peaceful years followed.

After the First World War, the Italians took over the Dodecanese, allegedly holding them in trust until they could be united with Greece. The new overlords also started excavating and restoring archaeological sites. By the 1930s their rule had become oppressive. They outlawed the Greek language and the Greek Orthodox religion. Rhodes was to be the playground for their ruling classes. When Mussolini fell Germany occupied the island until it was liberated by British troops in 1945. The Dodecanese were united with Greece in 1947.

Scratch Rhodes and you find history, ancient and modern, but the real treasure of the island is its people. Their generosity is famous. Their interest in visitors, legendary. In one restaurant our eight-year-old daughter asked for melon - not on the menu. We told her she couldn't have it, but the waiter shrugged, said 'No problem', and sent one of his lads to a supermarket to buy one. He charged the same price as the supermarket too. Our six-year-old son was intrigued by a poster showing various cocktails in a beach-side bar. He wanted a gin fizz complete with umbrellas, fruit and sparklers. The waiter said 'No problem' and produced a 'ginless fizz' with all the trimmings, for the cost of a coke. The point is, neither needed to go to the trouble of pandering to the children. We had practically convinced them they couldn't have their way.

And be prepared to answer questions about your family, home and job. They are not prying, well no more than normal in Greece, and they question everyone. They take the ancient law of hospitality seriously and show such an interest in the visitor that to a north European it may seem like prying. Don't be offended. Be flattered by the interest they show. In Greek the word for stranger and guest is the same.

William McDowall

RHODES

BAY OF TRIANDA

Ialyssos

Kremasti

Koskinou

Kalithea

Maritsa

Soroni

Faliraki

Kalithies

Faliraki

Afandou

Salakos

Afandou

BAY OF AFANDOU

Kritinia

Embonas

Tsambika

▲ Mt. Ataviros

Archangelos

Stegna

Agios Issidoros

Haraki

Laerma

Kalathos

Monolithos

Vliha

Lardos

Lindos

Lindos

Apolakia

Pefka

LARDOS BAY

Genadi

APOLAKKIA BAY

Katavia

CAPE PRASSONISSI

Rhodes - Pefka

KALITHEA BEACH 10 km S of Rhodes Town. Frequent buses.
Shower on beach, WCs in spa building. Food kiosk in season.
Good swimming in the beautifully clear water off the old spa. Three adjacent coves to choose from.

FALIRAKI BEACH 16 km S of Rhodes Town. Frequent buses.
Beach runs for 3.5 km, several access points. Large hotels on N section.
Facilities for watersports, showers, loungers for hire (200 Drs), tavernas.

AFANDOU BEACH 21 km S of Rhodes Town. Regular bus service.
A long, wide pebble and sand beach with an adjacent taverna. See **A-Z**.

TSAMBIKA BEACH 31 km S of Rhodes Town. Regular bus service.
A sheltered sandy beach with food, drink, pedaloes etc available in season.

STEGNA BEACH 36 km S of Rhodes. 3.5km from Archangelos.
Stegna is an attractive village strung out along the clean sandy beach. There is also a small harbour with fishing boats.

HARAKI BEACH 42.5 km S of Rhodes. Some buses in high season.
Sheltered beach and tavernas reached through olive groves dominated by ruins of Feraclos castle.

KALATHOS BEACH 49.5 km S of Rhodes Town.
A long shingle beach, still largely undeveloped.

VLIHA BEACH 54 km S of Rhodes Town.
A good sheltered beach. Tavernas in nearby hotels. Much less crowded than Lindos beach.

LINDOS BEACH 56 km S of Rhodes Town.
A wide sandy beach with clear water. Crowded in high season. See **A-Z**.

PEFKA BEACH 5 km S of Lindos.
Another sheltered sandy beach with showers and umbrellas for hire. There has been some villa development. Tavernas in the village.

Clystra - Rhodes

CLYSTRA BEACH 13 km S of Lindos. S end of Lardos bay.
Undeveloped sandy beach backed by dunes and pine trees. One taverna.

KIOTARI BEACH 18.5 km S of Lindos.
Fine shingle/coarse sand beaches with showers and good swimming although the beaches shelve steeply. Tavernas and bike rental kiosks.

GENADI BEACH 22 km S of Lindos.
Long (10 km) sand and shingle beaches which shelve steeply. The only development is three tavernas.

PLIMIRI BEACH 36 km S of Lindos.
Fine shingle beach with a jetty used for fishing from by the locals. One small taverna.

CAPE PRASSONISSI 49.5 km S of Lindos. 8.5 km down a rough track, turn off at Katavia.
A beautiful expanse of sand running between the island and the mainland. The south-east side is calm and has a taverna. Otherwise deserted.

APOLAKKIA BAY Approximately 80 km S of Rhodes Town.
A huge extent of undeveloped pebbly beach with superb views. Several access points between Katavia and Apolakia.

FOURNI BEACH 75.5 km S of Rhodes. Access from Monolithos.
Secluded, undeveloped sandy beach with nearby caves.

GLIFADAS BEACH 47 km S of Rhodes Town. 6 km from main road.
A remote rocky beach with nothing but a taverna and rooms to rent.

IALYSSOS BEACH 9 km S of Rhodes Town.
A sand and pebble beach with tavernas. Loungers and umbrellas for hire.

RHODES BEACH from aquarium to Elli beach and outer harbour.
Sand and pebbles, good swimming. Showers plus pedaloes, umbrellas and loungers for hire. Food and drink available. Very crowded!

SULEIMAN MOSQUE Sokratous St., Rhodes Old Town.
• Not open to visitors. Good views from adjacent clock tower.
A deep pink colour, built in honour of Suleiman the Magnificent after the Turkish conquest of 1522. See **WALK 2, A-Z**.

CHURCHES OF IALYSSOS Site of Ialyssos, Filerimos.
13 km SW of Rhodes. • Our Lady: Free on Mon., other days 200 Drs.
Within the ancient city are the Church of Our Lady of Filerimos, the underground Chapel of Ag. Georgios with its restored 15thC frescoes and a monastery with a Doric fountain. See **Filerimos.**

CATHEDRAL OF THE EVANGELIST Mandraki Harbour, Rhodes.
• 0730-1400, 1700-2030.
Built by the Italians in 1925 as a replica of the original Church of St John, which was destroyed in 1856, it has an ornate interior.

ST MARY'S CHURCH Ipoton St., Rhodes Old Town.
• 0830-1500. Closed Mon.
Now a Byzantine Museum, the plain high-ceilinged interior is an ideal setting for the frescoes etc exhibited there. See **WHAT TO SEE 1**.

MONI THARI 4 km SW of Laerma.
Bus at 1500 to Laerma. Ask in Laerma for the caretaker (Mr Anestes).
Beautiful setting in a hollow in the wooded hills. Several picnic sites in the surrounds. See **EXCURSION 4**.

MONI SKIADI 3 km down untarred road W of Messanagros.
Bus daily at 1500.
Byzantine monastery, in a superb setting, restored in the 18thC. Some interesting frescoes in the cupola. See **EXCURSION 4, A-Z**.

MONI TSAMBIKA 29 km S of Rhodes, 2.5 km off east coast road.
1.5 km up steep road to car park then rough path and concrete steps.
This tiny, white Byzantine monastery, only five cells, is set on a hilltop with superb views. It is the setting for an annual fertility-rite ceremony. See **EXCURSION 3, Tsambika Monastery.**

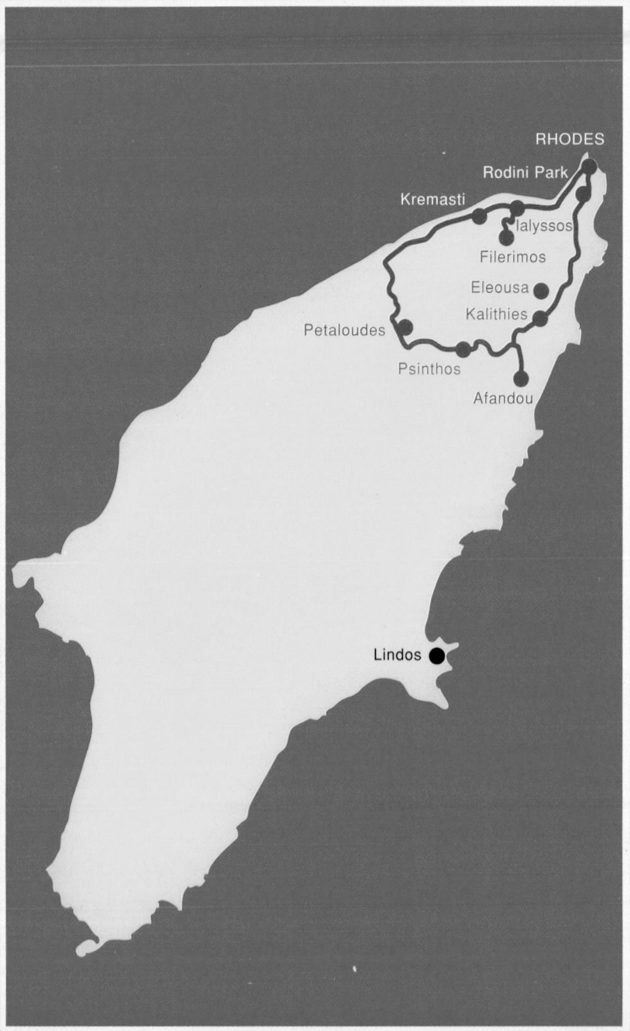

RHODES

Rodini Park

Kremasti

Ialyssos

Filerimos

Eleousa

Kalithies

Petaloudes

Psinthos

Afandou

Lindos

Petaloudes

(1 day). North island excursion. Take the west road out of Rhodes.

8 km: **Trianda** (now more commonly known as Ialyssos). Continue along the road past a stretch of hotels and modern buildings to arrive at Trianda, site of the most ancient remains on Rhodes (see **A-Z**). Visit the picturesque church of Theotokos - Mother of God - with its intricately carved icons.

Turn left from Trianda town centre and follow the winding road for 5 km up to Filerimos, site of the ancient city of Ialyssos (see **A-Z**). After visiting the church, chapel and monastery, return to the entrance, cross the car park and follow the Stations of the Cross along a shady walk to a viewpoint looking south to Paradisi and Kremasti.

Return to Trianda and turn left continuing along the coast road.

3 km: **Kremasti**. The modern Byzantine-style church was donated to the village by American expatriates. It can be visited if you track down the caretaker. This is also the site of several necropoles. See **A-Z**.

Turn left off the coast road after 6 km (the turning is well-signposted) and turn right after another 1 km.

7 km: **Petaloudes**. Leave the car in the car park at the entrance to the valley. The valley is very busy in season so get there early (see **A-Z**). After visiting the valley continue along the road in a south-east direction to the village of Psinthos. The road from Petaloudes to Psinthos is very rough but passes through dramatic mountainous countryside.

5 km: **Psinthos**. Site of a fierce battle early this century between the Turks and the Italians, ending nearly four centuries of Turkish rule.

10 km: **Kalithies**. From Psinthos continue towards Afandou but at 6 km leave the Afandou road on the right to continue left towards Kalithies where you will see an impressive view of Mount Psalida on the right. To the north of the village is Eleousa Monastery whose church is decorated with interesting frescoes. Check whether the monastery is open at the village of Kalithies.

12 km: **Rodini Park**. After driving through a modern industrial area on the outskirts of Rhodes Town, turn left off the main road into Rodini Park. The winding road leads through a tunnel in the rocks into the pleasant wooded park. The park is little-visited by tourists and is therefore very peaceful. There is an enclosure with deer, a children's playground, peacocks, and the Tomb of Ptolomies. See **A-Z**.

West Coast

(*1 day*). Take the west coast road passing through Ialyssos, Kremasti and past the airport to Kalamonas.

23 km: **Soroni**. This village is famous for its donkey races held on 30 July in honour of St Soulas. Continue along the coast road bearing right at Kalvarda and turn left after 4 km.

4 km: **Ancient Kamiros City** (see **A-Z**). The excavations give an excellent idea of what the city looked like, even though there is no interpretative information on site. You can, however, buy a guide book at the ticket kiosk or hire a guide (available in high season, price depends on number in the group). Spend a couple of hours exploring the site and then return to the main road.

13.5 km: **Kamiros Skala**, formerly known as Kritinia, a port founded by Cretan sailors. The ferry to Halki Island departs from here and there are three tavernas, making it a pleasant place to have a meal or drink.

4 km: **Kritinia Castle** (also known as Kamiros Castle). Turn right off the main road approximately 2 km after Kamiros Skala and follow the untarred road. The outer walls of the castle are in good repair but inside there is little to see apart from lizards sunning themselves on the rubble. However, there are splendid views of the neighbouring uninhabited islands of Makri and Strongli. Rejoin the main road south and pass through Kritinia and Amartos, bearing right.

19 km: **Siana**. Goblets with black figures dating from 6 BC were found in the necropolis here.

4 km: **Monolithos**. Continue south from this small village perched on the slopes of Mount Acramytis through pine forest. Follow the track leading to Monolithos Castle (2.5 km) with its amazing views of the sea and surrounding countryside (see **A-Z**). Leave your car in the car park and stroll up the stone steps to the castle. Inside is a tiny whitewashed chapel and the remains of a barrel vault of an earlier chapel. Drive another 4 km on down the untarred road to Fourni beach and the man-made caves in the limestone cliffs where Christians hid from the Arabs in the 7thC. Retrace the road through Monolithos village and Siana. 10.5 km further on from Siana, turn right for Embonas, the centre of the grape-growing region of Rhodes.

4 km: **Embonas**. This is one of the most picturesque villages on Rhodes and you can find guides for the climb up Mount Ataviros here. See **A-Z**.

After 9 km heading north, turn right. Climb the mountain road through pine trees and past the Alpine-style hotels (built for Italian commanders during the occupation) on Profitis Ilias, the third highest mountain on the island (see **A-Z**). In spring the area is carpeted with tiny white and pink anemone flowers. Return down to the main road, retrace it for 1 km then turn left for Apolona.

The road along the south edge of Profitis Ilias through to Apolona and Eleoussa is extremely scenic with pine-covered slopes which open out onto walnut and olive groves. At several points along the road there are picnic points, with rustic tables and chairs.

8 km: **Eleoussa**. At the centre of the village is an impressive yellow-washed colonnaded square. Unfortunately the village is occupied by the military and therefore no photographs are allowed. From Eleoussa, take a right turn and follow the road along the wide Loutani valley to the main east coast road at Kolimbia.

12 km: **Kolimbía**. At the main road take the left turn and return to Rhodes Town via Afandou and Faliraki.

RHODES

Kalithea

Faliraki

Afandou

Kolimbia

Epta Piges

Archangelos

Tsambika
Monastery

Feraclos
Castle

Lindos

Lindos

(1 day). Take the east coast road to Lindos.

10 km: **Kalithea**. Turn left off the coast road. This is the site of an abandoned thermal spa which was built by the Italians. Although the spa is now disused the site has considerable charm with its domed pool and palm trees. See **A-Z**.

15.5 km: **Faliraki**. An important beach resort with all sports facilities. The long sandy beach is lined by some of the island's largest hotels. An important ceramics factory, with a shop open to visitors, is here but otherwise the facilities cater almost entirely for the hotels and the beach and there is little sign of the original village. See **BEACHES 1**, **A-Z**. Turn right off the coast road at 5 km.

2 km: **Afandou**. This bustling village is the centre of carpet weaving on the island although otherwise there is little to see (see **A-Z**). On the other side of the main road is the turn for the beach and the golf course. Along the road to the course are the beginnings of a leisure complex planned to eventually include a swimming pool, tennis courts, hotels and restaurants. Rejoin the main road south.

6 km: **Kolimbia and Epta Piges**. From here follow the road alongside the usually dry riverbed of the Loutani Valley. After 2 km, take a steep left turn up a tarred road to a taverna and a car park. Raucous peacocks often strut in the car park. Find the tunnel entrance next to the river and follow it (waterproof footwear is advised!) through to the bright, blue-green lake which is fed by seven streams (hence *Epta Piges*), (see **A-Z**). The lake and dam were constructed by the Italians to feed irrigation aqueducts which can be seen beside the main road from Kolimbia to the coast. Return to Kolimbia and follow the road south to Tsambika Monastery. Tsambika Monastery is well worth a visit, though its spectacular hill-top location makes access quite difficult. A tarred road leads to a car park from where a rough path and stone steps lead into the monastery. See **CHURCHES**, **A-Z**.

4 km: **Archangelos**. This is one of the most important ceramic producing centres on Rhodes. The village also has a pleasant old quarter and a 15thC castle (see **A-Z**). Turn left off the road after 4 km.

4 km: **Feraclos Castle**. One of the most powerful castles of the Knights, with a panoramic sea view. Access is by rough track. Turn left 2 km after the turn off on the main road. There are wonderful views along the

coast although little remains of the castle itself. See **A-Z**.

Back on the main road turn left towards Lindos. About 4 km after the village of Kalathos the road sweeps round a corner giving a dramatic view of Lindos bay and the Acropolis towering above it.

18 km: **Lindos**. This is the second most important town on the island. It is dominated by the steep cliff on which stands the Acropolis of Lindos with its many points of interest. No traffic is allowed in the main square or the village itself so follow the signs to the car parks. See **LINDOS**, **A-Z**.

Return to Rhodes Town following the main road or follow **EXCURSION 4**.

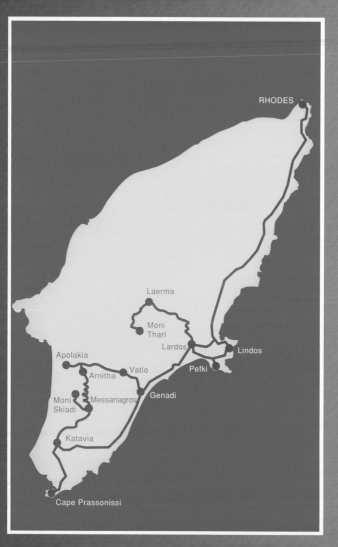

Lindos-south Rhodes

(1 day). Starting from Lindos take the small road south out of town to curve round Mount Marmari. Notice the chapel situated in a small pass. After the left turn to Pefki (4 km) the road gets rough. On the left is Lardos bay with 3 km of sandy beaches.

8 km: **Lardos**. See the ruins of a medieval castle. Take the south road out of Lardos and follow the signs for Laerma. The road takes a scenic route winding gently up a wooded hillside. In spring the grassy slopes are covered with an abundance of wild flowers, including a great variety of orchids.

12 km: **Laerma**. This is a picturesque hill village. Enquire here for the caretaker of Thari Monastery. Take an untarred rough road out of the village to the south west, following the signs to Profilia. After 2 km take the turn for the monastery which lies 2 km down another rough track.

4 km: **Moni Thari**. (See CHURCHES). The road between here and Profilia is very bad so return to Lardos and follow the coast road south. The road passes numerous pleasant sandy beaches, all emptier than the beaches in the more developed north of the island.

14 km: **Genadi**, last of the east coast resorts. Just before the village three windmills, similar in style to the famous ones at Mandraki, can be seen near the roadside. After Genadi the coastal plain widens out into a fertile agricultural area. Between Genadi and Katavia there is much evidence of the Italian occupation with many large, abandoned, fortified buildings.

19 km: **Katavia**. The 14/15thC church has 17thC frescoes and remains dating from the pre-Christian era have been found near the village. From here rough tracks lead to the island's most southerly point at Cape Prassonissi. After 8 km the track reaches the coast and there are breathtaking vistas of the windswept sandy causeway which joins a small island and Cape Prassonissi to the mainland.

Cape Prassonissi. Walk over the causeway to the island where a track leads past Italian fortifications to the lighthouse at the most southerly point of Rhodes.

Return to Katavia. Turn right at the main road and left up the unsurfaced road towards Messanagros. Although the road is rough and precipitous in places there are spectacular views to be had beyond Messanagros and the visit to Moni Skiadi makes it worth the effort.

12 km: **Messanagros**. Turn to Moni Skiadi (not very well signposted).
3 km: **Moni Skiadi**. See CHURCHES.
Return to Messanagros and take the left turn towards Arnitha and
Apolakia. The road climbs up along the Koukouliari ridge from where
panoramic views of both the east and west coasts are visible. Continue
through Arnitha to the main road and turn left for Apolakia.
15 km: **Apolakia**. A small, thriving village, surrounded by citrus and
walnut groves. See **A-Z**.
Retrace the route for 2 km and then follow the road through Vatio to
Genadi where you can rejoin the main east coast road to Lindos.

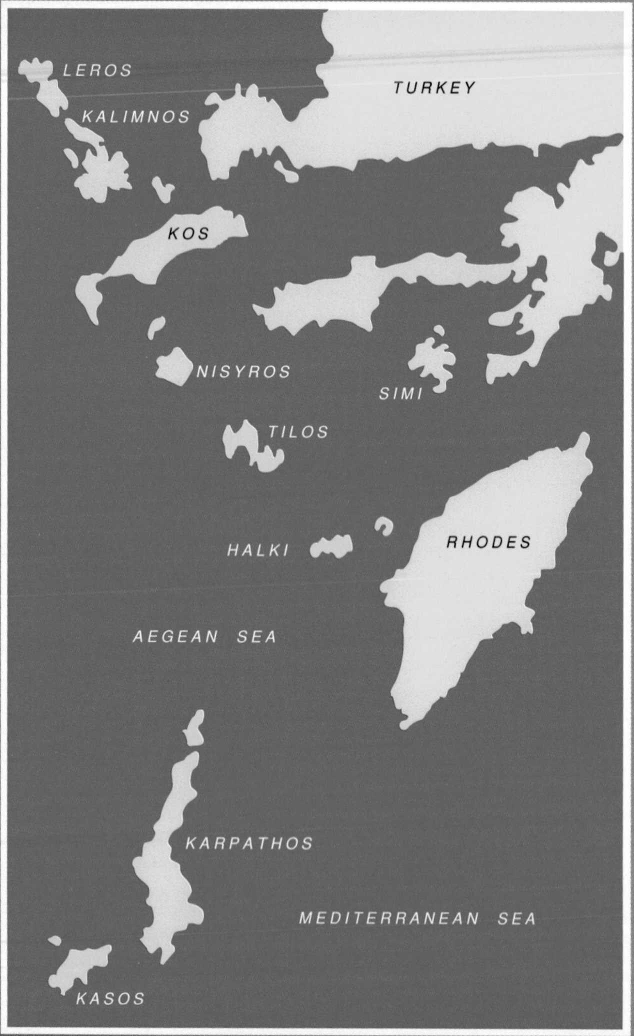

LEROS

KALIMNOS

TURKEY

KOS

NISYROS

SIMI

TILOS

HALKI

RHODES

AEGEAN SEA

KARPATHOS

MEDITERRANEAN SEA

KASOS

SIMI 40 km NW of Rhodes.
•Several daily boat services (1hr 15 min). Hydrofoil service takes 30 min but is expensive.
A pleasant day trip. The main port is a site of historical interest. See **A-Z**.

HALKI 50 km SW of Rhodes.
•Three boat links per week. Daily service from Kamiros Skala.
Closest island to Rhodes. A quiet island with pleasant beaches. See **A-Z**.

NISYROS 100 km W of Rhodes.
•Three boats a week in summer.
This island has an active volcano and a lush green landscape. See **A-Z**.

KOS 100 km NW of Rhodes.
•Daily ferries (4 hr). Hydrofoil service. Summer flights from Rhodes.
Second to Rhodes as a Dodecanese holiday destination. See **A-Z**.

KALIMNOS 135 km NW of Rhodes.
•One sailing daily, more in summer (6 hr).
A mountainous island with olive groves and orchards. See **A-Z**.

LEROS 150 km NW of Rhodes.
•Daily boat in summer (7 hr). Three flights a week on Mon., Wed., Fri.
Mountainous island with beautiful countryside. See **A-Z**.

KARPATHOS 50 km SW of Rhodes.
•Three ferries weekly (7 hr). Daily flights (35 min).
Good beaches, fertile valleys, rugged mountains and few tourists. See **A-Z**.

KASOS 170 km SW of Rhodes.
•Three boats weekly (10 hr). Six flights a week (30 min).
Scenic island with few tourist facilities. See **A-Z**.

TILOS 75 km W of Rhodes.
•Three ferries weekly.
Developing tourist island with a strong folk history. See **A-Z**.

Start from the Information kiosk in the main square - this is the setting down point for cars and coaches, which are not allowed in the town, therefore this is the point at which most people enter the village.

Go down the lane at the south end of the square. On the right is the donkey station, hire of a donkey for the ride up to the Acropolis will cost you 300 Drs plus 250 Drs for the return journey. If you decide to walk, follow the signposts for the Acropolis.

About 100 m on the left is the beautiful whitewashed Byzantine church of Panaghia, with its distinctive bell tower and red-tiled domes. The church is in full use and visitors are asked to dress respectably when entering the church. The plainness and simplicity of the courtyard contrast strongly with the richness of the decorated interior. The walls are completely covered by frescoes and on the east walls are icons decorated with silver, gilt and jewels.

Continue along the lane to the foot of the path to the Acropolis. There are women selling embroidered goods here. This is also a good place to look back onto the medieval houses clustered in a maze of lanes and alleys. The church of Panaghia is easily distinguished.

The entrance to the Acropolis (cost of entry 400 Drs) has a paved area with three massive stone cisterns for grain or water. At the foot of the steps up to the fortress is a huge Greek galley carved in relief in the rock. Go up the stairs into the Acropolis.

There are a mass of stone remnants in various states of preservation and restoration. The most prominent features are the Doric columns (c.208 BC) and the remains of the Temple of Athene Lindia. Unfortunately, long-term restoration work means that the columns are almost permanently covered in scaffolding.

Return towards the steps through the buildings added by the Knights in the 15thC when the Acropolis was turned into a fortress, and turn right immediately after the ticket booth, passing the donkey station. Hire a donkey or walk down the path to the village. The path gives wonderful views over Lindos Bay and the Grand Harbour. Visible on the headland on the opposite side of the bay is a circular stone tomb with a burial chamber. This is said to be the tomb of Kleouboulus, ruler of Lindos in the 6thC. From the path steps lead down to the beach, but continue on to the village. You will pass some fine carved doorways, typical of the

medieval houses of Lindos. Outside many of the houses are patterned black and white pebbled floors (*chochlaki*).

At the church of Panaghia walk south along the main shopping street of Lindos, also the location of most of the tavernas and bars in the town. Turn left in a small square at the end of the street and then first right along a lane which leads, in about 50 m, to an ancient stone amphi-theatre carved into the hill slope. This is a superbly atmospheric, well-preserved site.

Another 50 m further on there are dramatic views from the road of the nearly circular St Paul's Bay with the Acropolis towering above. The bay, reputed to be where St Paul landed on the island, has a pleasant small beach and a tiny chapel.

Follow the road on along the length of the bay and turn back uphill to Stavri Square. From here you get the best overall view of Lindos. Take the first left and follow the lane that skirts the hill of the Necropolis, on the west edge of the village, back to the main square.

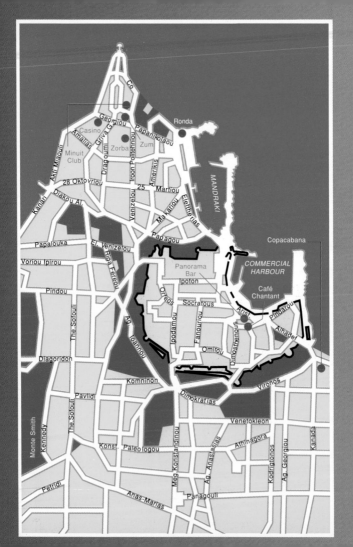

Rhodes Town

COPACABANA 4, Australias St.
• 2100-0230. • No entrance charge but drinks minimum of 1200 Drs.
Lively atmosphere. Singers from Rhodes and the Greek mainland are show-ered with carnation petals as a sign of appreciation. Mainly Greek clientele.

MINUIT CLUB 6 Kastelorizou St., New Town.
• 2200-0230.
Very popular. Friendly staff, and a lively atmosphere. A good mix of ages and nationalities. Greek music and folk dancing display at midnight.

CASINO Grand Hotel Astir Palace, New Town.
Roulette, baccarat. Evening wear and passport obligatory for entry.
One of only three casinos in all of Greece.

ZUM Georgiou Papanikolaou, New Town.
A noisy, lively bar, very popular with Scandinavians.

ZORBA Iroon Politechniou St., New Town.
• 2100-0230. • Min. charge 1200 Drs. Walking distance from centre.
Informal atmosphere and very popular with the locals.

RONDA Pl Koundourioti (in the Elli Club buildings), New Town.
• 2200-0230.
Greek and international music with artistes from all over Greece. Young clientele of various nationalities.

PANORAMA BAR Pl Ippocratous (Sindrivani Sq), Old Town.
• 2000-0230. • Moderate prices.
Friendly bar in picturesque setting on second and third floor terraces. Well-decorated with an abundance of plants. A good vantage point to watch the nightlife of the square.

CAFÉ CHANTANT off Pl Ippocratous (behind Panorama Bar).
• 2200-0230.
Greek music in a very atmospheric bar. Extremely popular with young Greeks.

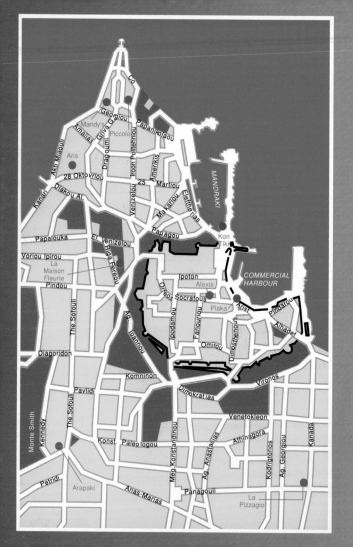

Rhodes Town

PLAKA Pl Ippocratous (Sindrivani Sq), Old Town.
• Moderate prices.
One of the best in Rhodes! Very friendly proprietor, superb views of the Old Town walls and the square. Wonderful fresh seafood.

ALEXIS Socratous St., Old Town.
• Expensive.
Mezes, fresh fish and seafood served in this luxurious restaurant set within a small courtyard.

LA PIZZAGIO Pl Kostaridi on Kanada.
• Moderate prices.
Try this popular pizza and pasta house for a change.

ARAPAKI Themistokli Sofouli.
• Reasonably priced, authentic Greek food.
Serves some dishes not available elsewhere and also good rice dishes.

KON TIKI floating platform, Mandraki Harbour.
Floating seafood restaurant. Very expensive but worth it for the setting.

LA MAISON FLEURIE Riga Fereou St., Old Town.
Opposite Amboise Gate.
French cuisine. Reasonable food but lacking in atmosphere.

ARIS 46 Georgios Leondos St., New Town.
• Open daytime and evening. • Moderately priced.
The emphasis is on Greek food in this restaurant. Very friendly proprietor.

PICCOLO 9 Kastellorizo St., New Town.
A wide variety of international dishes and a trio of musicians to provide atmosphere. Caters mainly for Scandinavians.

MANDY'S Patmou Chalkis, Old Town.
• 2000 Drs per person.
Excellent Chinese restaurant with dishes from a wide range of specialities.

TSAMPICOS Kavoyrakia Beach, 10 min by car or taxi out of Rhodes Town on Kalithea road. •Moderate prices.
Fresh seafood in this family-run beach taverna. Popular with Greeks at weekends and tourists from the local hotels.

CAS CASTELLANA 33 Aristotelous St., Old Town.
International menu with succulent seafood dishes served within this 15thC Knight's house and garden enclosed by ramparts.

PYTHAGORAS 22 Pythagoras St., Old Town.
A roomy family-run taverna with a cheerful atmosphere and fresh seafood.

ARGO Pl Ippocratous, Old Town.
•Moderate-expensive.
Steaks and seafood served in a lovely setting above the busy square.

HIPPOCRATES RESTAURANT Pythagoras St. (off Ippocarous).
•Moderate prices.
Greek food served at tables set out along the alleyway. Popular locally.

NISIROS TAVERNA 47-49 Ag. Fanouriou, Old Town.
•Moderate prices.
An authentic Old Town taverna serving Greek food in homely surroundings. Off the main tourist trail but just a brief walk from busy Socratous St.

LOUKOULOS 33 Amerikis St., New Town.
•A varied Greek menu at reasonable prices.
A small shady garden, sheltered from the noises of the street.

LINDOS ZACHAROPLASTEION 33 Amerikis St., New Town.
Coffee house with a wide variety of desserts - excellent creamy cakes and ice-creams - and a selection of coffees and teas. Well patronised by locals.

TZAKI 5.5 km from Rhodes Town at Ixia. (West coast road).
Reasonable prices and popular with tourists from nearby hotels, but frequented by Greeks too. Live Greek music.

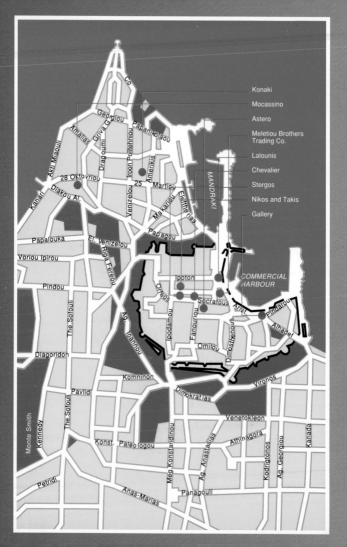

Konaki

Mocassino

Astero

Meletiou Brothers
Trading Co.

Lalounis

Chevalier

Stergos

Nikos and Takis

Gallery

MANDRAKI

COMMERCIAL
HARBOUR

Co.

Georgiou

Paraskefou

Amerikis

Anatfas

Griva G.

Diminotou

Troon Politehniou

28 Oktovriou

25

Diakou Al.

Venizelou

Martieu

25

Kanari

Akti Miaouli

Papalouka

El. Venizelou

Makariou

Eleftherias

Papagou

Voriou Ipirou

Pindou

Ipoton

Orfeos

Socratous

The Sofouli

Ag. Ioannou

Ipodamou

Fanourtou

Arieli

Pindarou

Alhadef

Diagoridon

Omirou

Dimostinous

Monte Smith

Kennedy

Pavlidi

The Sofouli

Komninon

Dimokratias

Vironos

Venetokleon

Konst. Paleologou

Meg Konstandinou

Ag. Anastasias

Athinagora

Kodrigtonos

Ag. Georgiou

Kanada

Petridi

Anas-Marias

Panagouli

KONAKI 55 Amerikis St., Rhodes New Town.
Tosita Foundation craftshop. The majority of the articles are produced by workers working from home. The high-quality pottery is definitely worth looking at.

MOCASSINO 28 Octovrou St., Rhodes New Town.
High-quality men's and women's shoes. Also handbags. Prices compare favourably with similar quality goods in Britain.

GALLERY 47-49 Martyron Evreon, Rhodes Old Town.
Gallery selling high-quality work by modern Greek artists, potters, weavers.

ASTERO 1 Fanagouriou St., Rhodes Old Town.
Shop selling old copperware including pots and decorated plates. Some rare pieces of work from the Dodecanese. Very reasonable prices.

MELETIOU BROTHERS TRADING COMPANY Ermou (just off Pl Ippocratous), Rhodes Old Town.
Moderately-priced, good-quality wooden craftware, some in Turkish style.

LALOUNIS Pl Moussiou, Rhodes Old Town.
The famous Athens jewellers with a select choice of very high quality pieces - inspirations or reproductions from Ancient Greece. Cheaper than the Paris or Zurich shop but still very expensive. Wonderful medieval atmosphere.

CHEVALIER 96 Socratous St., Rhodes Old Town.
Hand-made carpets from all over Greece, some of them depicting scenes from Greek mythology.

STERGOS 4 Panetiou St., Rhodes Old Town.
A jewellers but also selling a wide selection of fossils, crystals and semi-precious polished stones. Expensive!

NIKOS and TAKIS Panetiou St., Rhodes Old Town.
Quality clothing with a flavour of Rhodes in both design and colours.

SHOPPING 2

PANERI 1 Fanouraki St., Rhodes New Town.
A shop selling health foods, organically grown produce, Greek herbs and natural cosmetics. The proprietor is a friendly Greek-American.

GALLURAKIS 100 Griva St., Rhodes New Town.
A good selection of leather goods (bags, belts, sandals etc) at very reasonable prices.

CHRISTOS Griva St., Rhodes New Town.
Water colours of Rhodian countryside and sights displayed in a garden courtyard. Customers can enjoy a drink while browsing.

ROYAL MINK Apellou (just off Pl Moussiou), Rhodes Old Town.
Traditional design rugs and carpets. A weaver works at a loom on the premises.

PHIDIAS Panetiou St., Rhodes Old Town.
Pottery from Athens and hand painted by Costas Peppas. Both antique copies and his own inspirations.

H. MEVLOUTAKI 149 Socratous St., Rhodes Old Town.
A shop in a busy bazaar area of the Old Town selling leather sandals of every description.

HARTOFILIS 81 Socratous St., Rhodes Old Town.
Shop selling embroidered articles from all over Greece and Cyprus and blouses from Rhodes. Handkerchiefs, tablecloths, table mats and serviettes each showing the technique from a particular region.

MEDITERRANEA BORSE 21 Parados Socratous, Old Town.
A small workshop run by three young Italians, producing unusual, well-designed bags and belts. Very good value.

COSMOS Ermou (just off Pl Ippocratous), Rhodes Old Town.
High-quality furs sold fom this shop which has a friendly and knowledgable proprietor.

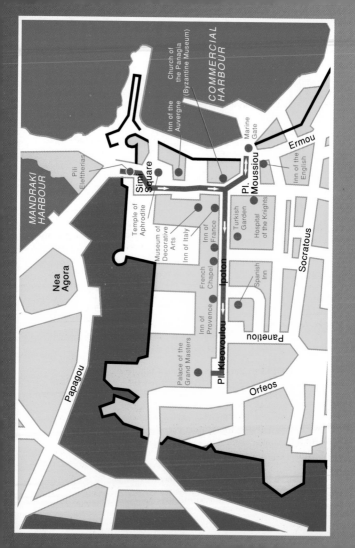

MANDRAKI HARBOUR

COMMERCIAL HARBOUR

Church of the Panagia (Byzantine Museum)

Inn of the Auvergne

Marine Gate

Ermou

Inn of the English

Plii Eleftherias

Simi Square

Temple of Aphrodite

Pl. Moussiou

Museum of Decorative Arts

Inn of Italy

Inn of France

Turkish Garden

Hospital of the Knights

Socratous

Nea Agora

French Chapel

Ipoton

Spanish Inn

Inn of Provence

Pl. Kleovoulou

Panetiou

Papagou

Palace of the Grand Masters

Orfeos

Knight's Quarter

(*3 hr*) From Mandraki Harbour enter the city through the Pili Eleftherias (Gate of Freedom). This gate is approached across the moat where a herd of Rhodian deer can be seen. Opposite the gate, at the other end of Simi Square are the remains of a temple to Aphrodite (often obscured by the amount of traffic from the harbour passing to and fro through the square) and behind this is the Inn of the Auvergne Knights. This was built in the 15thC and renovated around 1919 and overlooks Argirokastrou Square. In the centre of Argirokastrou is a Byzantine font which forms the base of a fountain decorated by a small dolphin. All round the square are mounds of stone cannonballs dating from the 15thC. The Institute of History and the Museum of Decorative Arts (see **A-Z**) are also located in this square.

Pass under an arch and you will see on the left the Byzantine church of Panagia (St Mary) which houses the Byzantine Museum. Leaving Ipoton on the right continue to Platia Moussiou and the Inn of the English, founded in 1482. On the left stands the impressive Marine Gate, through which can be seen the commercial harbour. This 15thC gate bears the coat of arms of the Grand Master Pierre d'Aubusson. Opposite is the Hospital of the Knights founded in 1440 and which now houses the Archaeological Museum (see **WHAT TO SEE 1**).

Go back and turn left up Ipoton Street (or the **Avenue of the Knights**) which leads to the Palace. The buildings were sympathetically restored in the early part of this century exactly as they were in medieval times and the cobbled street is very atmospheric. Along this street are four of the remaining six Inns. On the left is the north facade of the Hospital and, opposite, the Italian Inn. Further along on the right is the Inn of France - the most elegant of all and next to it the small French chapel with the statue of Our Lady with the Saviour and the French Lilies. Across from the French Inn, behind a wrought-iron gate, is a cool, shady Turkish garden.

Next to the French Inn is the Inn of Provence and, opposite, the Spanish Inn. Pass under the arch to arrive at the castle square, Platia Kleovoulou. This used to be the site of the church of St John, destroyed by an explosion when gunpowder was ignited by a lightning strike. The Palace of the Grand Masters is on the right and ahead the square opens onto Orfeos Street and the Turkish Quarter.

The Old Town

(*2/3 hr*) Starting from the Suleiman Mosque (see **CHURCHES**), opposite is the Turkish Library, surrounded by a small paved garden. It contains a Koran of the 15/16thC with illuminations.

Follow Socratous Street, the old bazaar, where houses and shops still keep something of the Turkish atmosphere, downhill towards Hippocrates Square. At the opposite side of the square is the Municipal Library, notice the intricately decorated first floor windows. At the centre of the square is a fountain, decorated with green and blue tiles, and a small minaret. Now take Aristotelous Street which leads to the Square of the Jewish Martyrs where Germans rounded up all the Jews in 1944 and deported them. In the centre there is a fountain decorated with bronze sea horses. The Admiralty Palace, the former residence of the Archbishop, stands on one side of the square.

Pindarou Street passes the ruins of the Gothic church of St Marie du Bourg and the hospice of St Catherine before arriving at St Catherine's Gate. The gate overlooks the busy Commercial Harbour.

Walk towards the Tower of Italy through an area devoid of all signs of tourism and follow the ramparts west along Ekatonos Street and. Tlipolemou Street. This will take you past the small 14thC church of St Catherine (a Byzantine church converted to a mosque by the Turks but now a church again). Opposite St Catherine's church is St Trinity Church, an unusually-shaped 15thC church, also once a mosque.

Turn left past this church towards the city ramparts where you will see the small church of St John the Baptist in the rampart walls. Turn right into Aristomenous Square. Here excavations reveal the remains of a mill, with several mill stones visible. Bear left towards the dilapidated St Kyriaki church (renamed Bourouzan).

Go down Omirou Street. A walk along this narrow street gives something of the flavour of the Turkish Quarter and is a pleasant escape from the main tourist trail on Socratous Street. Opposite No.31 there is a gateway leading to Retjep Pasha Mosque, once very grand, now run-down and closed (see **CHURCHES**). Opposite is Aghios Fanourios Church with 13th and 15thC frescoes. Cross over Ag Fanoutiou Street and turn right towards open-air Folk Dance Theatre (see **Cultural Events**). The street opposite the entrance leads to Arionos Square. On the left you have the Turkish baths and on the right the mosque of Sultan Mustafa.

New Town

(*3 hr*) Starting at the aquarium in the gardens on the northern tip of the island. Leave the gardens and take the Co road along the beach on the north-east side of town. The road leaves the beach and runs along the railings of gardens in which is the abandoned Hotel of the Roses. This once luxurious hotel was built during the Italian occupation and it was here that the peace treaty between Israel and Egypt was signed. Today it lies empty, the property of the town of Rhodes.

Turning left into Vas Konstantinou will lead you to the gates of the Hotel of the Roses, and then to the Turkish cemetery next to the tiny Murad Reis Mosque. Murad Reis was the naval commander of the Turkish fleet during the 1522 seige and the mosque is just about big enough for his tomb. The cemetery contains graves of various notable characters many of whom were exiles in Rhodes - *eg* Vizirs, Pashas, a Shah of Persia and the poet Mohammed Ahmed Ephendi. Tombstones with a turban are those of men, plain ones are women. The cemetery is now somewhat neglected but is shady and peaceful.

Leaving the cemetery onto Platia Koundourioti you are in the Mandraki port area. The entrance of the harbour is maked by two columns bearing bronze deer - the emblem of Rhodes. This was supposedly the site of the Colossus of Rhodes (though it is more likely to have been at the Acropolis, Monte Smith). Walking down Eleftherias along the seafront you'll pass the grandiose buildings of the harbour. On your right is the National Theatre, which sometimes serves as a cinema, and opposite is the Town Hall which is built in impressive Venetian Gothic style and was once used as the Governor's Palace. On your left is the square bell tower of the Cathedral of St John the Evangelist (see **CHURCHES**). The fountain in the front is a replica of Viterbo. Opposite is the post office and further down on the right are the city courts. Moored along the harbour are large yachts from all over Europe, some available for charter. This is also where several of the boats for the islands leave from and there are stalls and small boats offering sponges for sale.

Finally you arrive at Nea Agora (new market) a huge, irregular heptagonal building of Turkish style enclosing a courtyard with cafés, shops and market stalls. Walking along the jetty you will pass three mills that used to grind the flour for the medieval cargo ships. At the end of the jetty is the Fort of St Nicholas, now a lighthouse. See **Mandraki.**

Palace of the
Grand Masters

Avenue of the
Knights

Ramparts

Municipal Art
Gallery

Museum of
Decorative Arts

Byzantine Museum

Archaeological Museum

Turkish Quarter

Jewish Quarter

MANDRAKI

COMMERCIAL
HARBOUR

Co

Georgiou

Papanikolaou

Amalias

Griva G.

Dragoumi

Iroon Politehniou

Amerikis

Akti Miaouli

28 Oktovriou

Venizelou

25

Martiou

Elefther
ias

Kanari

Diakou Al.

Makariou

Papagou

Papalouka

El. Venizelou

Voriou Ipirou

Pindou

Ipoton

Oreos

Socratous

Anst.

Pindarou

The Sofouli

Diagoridon

Ipodamou

Fanouriou

Omirou

Dimosthenous

Alhadet

Komninon

Ag. Ioannou

Dimokratias

Vironos

Monte Smith

Kennedy

Pavlidi

The Sofouli

Konst. Paleologou

Venetokleon

Kodrigionos

Ag. Georgiou

Kanada

Petridi

Meg. Konstandinou

Ag. Anastasias

Athinagora

Anas-Marias

Panagouli

Rhodes Town

PALACE OF THE GRAND MASTERS Pl Klevoulou, Old Town.
•0800-1500. Closed Mon. •300 Drs.
More a fortress than a palace. Home of the leader of the Knights . See **A-Z**.

AVENUE OF THE KNIGHTS (ODHOS IPOTON) Old Town.
*Narrow, cobbled street leading up to the Palace of the Grand Masters. On
either side are the Inns of the various orders of Knights. See* **A-Z**.

THE RAMPARTS Old Town.
•Guided tours 1445 Tues., Sat. •300 Drs.
Superb, awesome fortifications, built by the Knights. See **Walls**.

ARCHAEOLOGICAL MUSEUM Pl Moussiou, Old Town.
•0830-1500. Closed Mon. •300 Drs.
Exhibition of archaeological finds, labelled in Greek and English.

MUSEUM OF DECORATIVE ARTS Pl Argirokastrou, Old Town.
•0830-1500. Closed Mon. • 200 Drs.
Beautiful furniture, costumes, pottery, many items from Lindos. See **A-Z**.

MUNICIPAL ART GALLERY Pl Simi, Old Town.
•0730-1430. 1700-2300 Wed. •150 Drs.
*A modern building constructed in a medieval style. Local artists are featured
in modern art exhibitions.*

BYZANTINE MUSEUM Port end of Ipoton St., Old Town.
•0830-1500. Closed Mon. •300 Drs.
Once the Knights' cathedral and a mosque under Turkish rule. See **WALK 1**.

TURKISH QUARTER Old Town.
*The Turkish influence, which can be seen in the numerous minarets and
arched windows, dates from the 16thC. See* **CHURCHES**, **A-Z**.

JEWISH QUARTER Old Town.
*The prominent feature of the area (SE part of the Old Town) is the fountain
in the Square of the Jewish Martyrs topped by bronze sea horses. See* **A-Z**.

Monte Smith
RHODES
BAY OF TRIANDA
Ialyssos
Kremasti ● ● Koskinou
Filerimos
Soroni ● Maritsa ● Thermae
Kalithea
Petaloudes ● Kalithies ●
Kamiros/Ancient Kamiros Faliraki
Salakos ● Afandou ●
Kamiros Castle *BAY OF AFANDOU*
Kritinia ●
Embonas ●
▲ *Mt. Ataviros* Archangelos ●
Agios Issidoros ●
Laerma ● Feraclos Castle
Monolithos ●
Monolithos Castle
Lardos ● Lindos
APOLAKKIA BAY Apolakia ● *LARDOS BAY*
Genadi ●
Katavia ●
CAPE PRASSONISSI

Island

LINDOS 56 km S of Rhodes Town on E coast.
*Quaint narrow streets and white houses plus the famed Acropolis of Lindos.
See* **EXCURSION 3, A-Z** .

KAMIROS 34 km SW of Rhodes Town on W coast.
•0830-1500. Closed Mon. 3 buses daily. •200 Drs.
*A huge excavated site. The main street leads uphill to the Temple of Athena
and on either side are alleyways of houses. See* **EXCURSION 2, A-Z.**

FILERIMOS 15 km SW of Rhodes Town.
•0830-1500. Closed Mon. •200 Drs.
The site of the ancient city of Ialyssos. See **CHURCHES, EXCURSION 1, A-Z**

PETALOUDES 25 km SW of Rhodes Town.
•0830-1700. •100 Drs mid-June to Sept.
Wooded valley, home to hundreds of brightly coloured butterflies. See **A-Z**.

MONOLITHOS CASTLE 2 km from Monolithos, SW of Island.
Daily bus. Check Sun. •Free.
*Ruined castle on a rock outcrop. The sweeping views are majestic but
beware of the unguarded 265 m drop! See* **A-Z**.

MONTE SMITH 1.5 km W of Rhodes Town.
*Site of main visible classical remains of Ancient Rhodes town. Named after
an English admiral who used it as a look-out point. See* **Ancient Rhodes**.

FERACLOS CASTLE 40 km S of Rhodes Town on E coast.
*Used by the Knights as a fortress/prison this was the last fortification to fall
to the Turks. Impressive views of the east coast. See* **EXCURSION 3, A-Z**

KAMIROS CASTLE On road to Kritinia. 50 km SW of Rhodes .
*Ruins, with coats of arms of Grand Masters on walls. Superb views of the
west coast. See* **EXCURSION 2**.

THERMAE KALITHEA 12 km S of Rhodes Town.
Disused spa built by the Italians in the 1920s in an Arabic style. See **A-Z**.

Accidents and Breakdowns: Standard procedure should be employed if unfortunate enough to be involved in a road accident. That is, exchange of name and insurance details. The police are unlikely to intervene unless someone has been injured in which case it is wise to contact your Consulate.

Car hire agencies will supply emergency service details in the event of the breakdown of one of their vehicles. Road Assistance tel: 104.

Accommodation: Rhodes Town and the west coast are the principal sites of hotel accommodation. A detailed list of hotels is available from the office of the *Association of Hotels, Rhodes,* located behind the tourist office in Makariou Street. The tourist office itself can advise on accommodation but cannot make reservations. Hotel categories range from Luxury (Lux) through to family run accommodation (D or E). There are no hotels in Lindos but there are plenty of rooms to let, most of good quality. The Tourist Information office in the main square in Lindos will give you details and arrange booking. *Domatia* (private houses) provide good and, usually, cheap accommodation. Details of these establishments can be obtained from the Tourist Police. See also **Camping**.

Afandou: 20 km from Rhodes. The town could not be seen off the coast by marauding pirates, hence the name of Afandou which means 'invisible'. The main industry of this commercial town is carpet weaving. There is a pleasant beach nearby. Also nearby is the only golf course on the island. See **BEACHES 1**.

Airport: Rhodes International Airport is located at Paradisi 12 km along the west coast road from Rhodes Town. The airport has all the usual facilities of an international airport including a tourist office. Travel to Rhodes Town is by bus or taxi. The Olympic Airways bus service is preferable to the local buses as the Olympic buses have greater luggage capacity. Taxis are fast, reasonably priced and plentiful.

Ancient Rhodes: Situated 2 km outside Rhodes Town.
The ancient Hellenistic town of Rhodes located on the eastern slopes of Monte Smith. There are some remains of the town including a reconstructed stadium and the partially restored temple of Apollo. The hill, originally known as Mount Ag. Stephanos, has been known as Monte Smith since the time of the Napoleonic Wars when the English Admiral, Sydney Smith, used it as an observation point. See **WHAT TO SEE 2**.

Apolakia: Almost the last inhabited spot on the west coast of the island, situated some 91 km from Rhodes Town. The Church of Aghios Georghios Vardas on the outskirts of the village is said to be the oldest church in the Dodecanese.

Archangelos: Considered the largest village on the island. Located some 33 km from Rhodes Town on the east coast road and within a fertile area, it is the centre of the main citrus-growing region on the island. The town itself contains an atmospheric old quarter. The village lies in the shadow of a 15thC fortress commissioned by Grand Knight Master Orsini. There are many cobblers in the village producing leather boots, originally worn as protection against snakes.

Astipalia: The most westerly of the Dodecanese Islands in a remote position between Kos and the Cycladic island of Amorga.

Avenue of the Knights (Odhos Ipoton): Restored to reflect its original appearance from the time when the Knights of St John were the rulers of Rhodes. This cobbled street contains no shops and no traders. At one end is the resplendently restored Palace of the Grand Masters (see **A-Z**) which dates from the 14thC, and at the other is the Hospital of the Knights.

Along its length are the Inns (see **A-Z**) which were the quarters for each of the seven sections of the Knights (with the exception of England and Auvergne). These sections were known as Tongues and each represented a different part of medieval Europe and was responsible for defending a different section of the ramparts. See **Knights**, **Walls**.

Babysitting: Certain hotels may be able to arrange child minding services if given sufficient advance notice. Children usually stay up late and are accepted in most establishments.

Banks: Open 0800-1400 Mon.-Fri. and Sat. mornings for exchange. (See **Public Holidays**). *National Bank of Greece*, Kypros Square; *Commercial Bank of Greece*, Eleftherias Square; *Credit Bank of Greece*, Kypros Square. See **Money**.

Bicycle and Motorbike Hire: Although bicycles can be hired many of the sites of interest on the island are not reachable within a day's cycling.

Mopeds for hire in Rhodes usually include only third party insurance which does not cover damage to either the rider or the bike. Full insurance is therefore advisable as some of the roads to the south of the island can be hazardous. Hire shops, for both cycles and motorbikes, can be found throughout Rhodes Town, at Faliraki, Trianda, Lindos and several smaller beaches. A bike costs around 300 Drs/day and a moped 2500 Drs/day. No licence required up to 125cc. Motorbikes are not allowed in towns between 1400 and 1630 or after 2300.

Boat Services: The main passenger ferry port is the Commercial Harbour located to east of the Old Town. There are scheduled stopping services to all of the Dodecanese Islands (see **ISLANDS**) as well as to Piraeus, Crete and Turkey. The journey time varies depending on the number of ports of call. There is a speedier hydrofoil service, known as the Flying Dolphin, with services in high season to Kos, Simi and Patmos. At present there is a free service to Kastellorizo as the Greek government are trying to promote tourism there.

From Mandraki Harbour there are excursion and day-trip sailings, these include services to other parts of Rhodes Island including Lindos. Contact the Tourist Office for details of where to obtain information about the various ferry operators, their schedules and their prices.

Bouzouki: *Bouzouki* music has experienced a revival over the last thirty years. The instrument was brought to Greece in the 1920s by

refugees from Asia Minor. It was banned at this time though there were several underground *bouzouki* clubs in Athens. Today the *bouzouki* characterizes Greek music, especially the old songs known as *rebetika*.

Budget:
Breakfast from 240 Drs per person.
Lunch in a restaurant from 750 - 800 Drs per person (*eg* Greek salad, beefburger, chips and a beer or Coke).
From 3500 Drs for a double room in 'C' category hotel, low season.
About 450 Drs per person in a camp site per day.
Theatre - from 1000 Drs per person.
Discos - minimum entrance 500 Drs per person.
Museums - from 200 Drs.

Buses: These are the cheapest method of travelling around the island. The three main departure points in Rhodes are as follows:
Eleftherias Square (opposite market) for routes inside town. Buses do a circuit every half hour but the town is so small that distances are easily walked (apart from that to Monte Smith); *Papagou Street* (KTEL buses) for east coast; *Averof Street* (RODA buses) for west coast.
Within the city limits a ticket costs 50 Drs and a day pass is available for 350 Drs. Rhodes-Lindos costs 330 Drs one way. Tickets are bought on the bus before departure. The usual bus services do not apply on Sundays and holidays, and in the high season buses get very crowded.

Cameras and Photography: Films, batteries and video tapes are available from photographic kiosks, music shops and larger stores (although items tend to be more expensive from the latter). Photography is allowed in most museums. **NB:** Because of the proximity to Turkey there is a large military presence on Rhodes, be careful to observe the 'No Photography' signs.

Camping: Unauthorized camping is forbidden on the island. There are two camping sites with all amenities including shops, sports facilities and their own nightlife. These are St George's Camping at Lardos Village 9 km from Lindos and at Faliraki Camping outside Faliraki

Village. Cost is about 450 Drs per person per day. See **Accommodation**.

Car Hire: Renting a car is an ideal method of visiting all the island's sites and sights at leisure. In summer it is advisable to book at least one day in advance. Most of the major agencies are represented in Rhodes Town. In addition there are many local agencies which may offer discounts. Local hire details include a minimum age of 23, presentation of a valid international licence and, occasionally, presentation of a passport.
It is advisable to ensure that comprehensive insurance is taken out. Many agencies require an accident damage deposit of up to 12,000 Drs. Major agencies usually waive this deposit if payment is made by credit card. Some agencies also have restrictions concerning driving on mountain roads, check for this.

Chemists: Known as *Pharmakia* and can be identified by their sign of a red or blue cross on a white background. As a rota system is in operation there is always one chemist open at any point of the day or night. The name and address of the duty chemist can be obtained from the hotel desk or by contacting the Tourist Police.

Cinemas: Several are to be found in the New Town. General release films are regularly shown with subtitles in Greek.

Climate: Rhodes is the island of Apollo, the Sun God. As befits this title, eight months of sunshine are usually recorded between April and January. February and March are considered rainy months. In spring and autumn the temperature drops considerably at night but is pleasant during the day. In the summer temperatures can soar on the east coast whilst the west coast tends to be cooler due to the northerly breeze.

Colossus of Rhodes: This 40 m statue, dedicated to the people of Rome, was considered one of the seven ancient wonders of the world. It was destroyed by an earthquake in 225 BC. Contrary to popular belief, it was located in the temple of Zeus at the Acropolis of Rhodes and did not bestride the harbour entrance at Mandraki.

Complaints: In the event of a general complaint about a hotel or restaurant then the Tourist Police can be contacted to arbitrate. Tel: 27423. See **Police**.

Consulates:
Great Britain - 23 25th March St., Rhodes Town. Tel: 27306/27247.
USA - c/o Voice of America Radio, Rhodes. Tel: 24180.
Australia - 15 Messogion Av, Athens. Tel: 775-7651.
Canada - 4 Ioann. Gennadiou St., Athens. Tel: 723-9511.
Republic of Ireland - 7 Vas. Konstandinou Av, Athens. Tel: 723-2771.
New Zealand - 15-17 Tsocha St., Athens. Tel: 641-0311-5.

Conversion Charts:

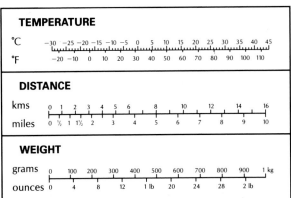

Crime and Theft: Greeks are, on the whole, very honest people, however the general rules of caution apply. Always keep money, travellers cheques and passports in a safe place such as the hotel safe. In the event of theft contact the police at Ethelondon Dodekanissiou, Rhodes New Town, tel: 27423.

Cultural Events: Enjoy the colourful costumes of the Folk Dance Theatre group located at Andronikou Street in the Old Town (season starts 1 May). The authentic atmosphere is further enhanced by the open air stage being designed to reflect the courtyard of a village house. Descriptive texts on the dances to be seen can be obtained at the entrance. Although slightly expensive at 1200 Drs it is an interesting spectacle.

Ancient Greek tragedies and comedies are enacted by the Dodecanese Theatre Company at, appropriately enough, the Ancient Theatre on Monte Smith. The season's programme also includes modern plays as well as classical, contemporary and folk music recitals. Details can be obtained from the NTOG office.

The *Son et Lumière* (Sound and Light) show takes place in a municipal garden behind the Place of the Grand Masters (entrance on Papagou St., opposite the New Market). The hour-long show gives an account of the Turkish seige of Rhodes in 1522. Performances in English take place daily (apart from Sat.) check the notice on the gates for times which vary from day to day in the high season. The cost is around 400 Drs.

Currency: The unit of currency is the drachma. There are 1, 2, 5, 10, 20, and 50 Drs coins and 50, 100, 500, 1000 and 5000 Drs notes. As the design has recently been changed there are currently different 1, 2 and 50 Dr coins in circulation.

Customs:

Duty Paid Into:	Cigarettes	or	Cigars	or	Tobacco	Spirits	Wine
E.E.C.	300		75		400 g	1.5 l	5 l
U.K.	300		75		400 g	1.5 l	5 l

Dodecanese: The name means 12 islands but as such is something of an anomaly as the group actually consists of 14 islands. The islands are closer to Turkey than to Greece and in ancient times were more influenced by the events of Asia Minor rather than Athens or Sparta. Achaens, Porians, Crusaders, Turks and then the Italians have all occupied the islands, which did not actually unite with Greece until after the German occupation during the Second World War. In addition to Rhodes, the main group of islands includes Kos, Kalimnos, Leros and Patmos which have regular ferry links to Piraeus and an inter-island hydrofoil service. The smaller islands - Karpathos, Kastelerizo, Halki, Simi, Tilos, Nisyros, Astipelea, Telendos and Lipsi are served by local ferries or excursion boats. Kos, Rhodes and Leros have airports. See **ISLANDS** and also individual **A-Z** entries.

Drinks: In the past Rhodian wines were famous throughout the Greek world. They are still of good quality especially the dry white Ilios or the dry red Chevalier de Rhodes.
Retsina is the wine of Greece itself. A pine-resin flavoured white wine

which is something of an acquired taste. Also something of an acquired taste is *ouzo*, an aniseed spirit usually drunk with water added. Metaxa is a Greek brandy and is generally sweeter than the French equivalent. The local *eau de vie* is called *oumi* and is similar to *raki* found in other parts of Greece. Lager type beers are popular, the Greek brand being Fix. Tap water is good. Coffee is always served with a glass of water. A request for coffee will usually result in instant coffee, *nes,* except in country areas where Greek (Turkish) coffee will be served. When ordering specify: *nes,* instant; *filtro,* filtered; *elliniko,* Greek. The latter is strong and served in tiny cups, it can be drunk *gliko* (sweet), *metrio* (medium), or *sketo* (plain).

Driving: An EEC or International Diving Licence and third party insurance are obligatory. Green card insurance is recommended. Use of seat belts is compulsory. There are two main routes on the island. The east coast road through Lindos and down past Katavia is tarred and in good condition. The west coast road through Ialyssos, Kamiros to Katavia is tarred but there are several sharp bends. A network of smaller roads links the two main routes but very few of these are tarred so low speeds and care are needed. The island is well signposted only on the main east and west coast roads and a road map is therefore essential. There are petrol stations in Rhodes Town, along main roads and in villages. They close at 1900 but one remains open on a rota basis. The address of the open station can be found in the local paper or at the taxi rank.

Drugs: The Greeks do not differentiate between hard and soft drugs and are quite strict on persons carrying even small amounts of hashish. Drug trafficking can mean life imprisonment.

Eating Out: There is no shortage of eating places in Rhodes Town and everyone should find something to suit their taste and their pocket. Possibilities range from *haute cuisine* in one of the upmarket tourist hotels to *souvlaki,* bought from a stall and eaten on the street. Expect to pay, very approximately, 800-1000 Drs for a meal listed as 'Cheap' on the Restaurants Topic page, 1000-2000 Drs for a meal listed as 'Medium' and 2000+ for an 'Expensive' meal. Prices are per person.

Epta Piges (Seven Springs): The site of an artificial lake, fed by seven streams, and a man-made waterfall designed to provide water for the irrigation canals of Kolombia which were introduced by the Italians in the 1930s. The area, which is about 30 km south of Rhodes Town, is extremely scenic and popular with tourists. See **EXCURSION 3**.

Electricity: The voltage is 220 Volts. An adapter is recommended for travellers from the UK.

Embonas: A picturesque village situated on the north-west slopes of Mount Ataviros in a tobacco and grape growing region. Tavernas in the area serve jugs of the local wine. Here you will also find guides for the ascent of Mount Ataviros. The other local attraction is the permanent dance troupe of villagers in traditional costume who participate in both small village fetes and larger national ones. At Embonas performances are organized during the last three weeks of August. See **EXCURSION 2**.

Emergencies: Police - Tel: 100; Fire - Tel: 199; Ambulance -Tel: 166; Hospital Emergency - Tel: 2555; Breakdown- Tel: 104; Tourist

Police - Tel: 27423. See **Health ,Crime and Theft.**

Events: *February*: Carnival with floats and fancy dress at Rhodes, Archangelos, Apolona and Kamiros Skala.
7 March: Union Day - the celebrations to mark the Dodecanese Islands becoming part of Greece.
First Monday of Lent: A fasting day when some eat only potatoes and garlic.
Good Friday: Silent processions through the town.
Easter Saturday: Evening mass and fireworks and candles at midnight.
1 May: Doorways decorated with garlands of flowers.
June: The last ten days mark the summer celebrations with beauty competitions, folk dancing and singing with the participation of tourists.
July: The first week is naval week with boat races, open air concerts and fireworks. At the end of the month there is a religious festival with athletics at Aghios Soulas near Soroni on the west coast.
August: An exhibition of arts and crafts at Kremasti with processions and dancing on Assumption Day (15 August). This is the biggest festival in the Dodecanese and lasts for one week.
8 September: Nativity of the Virgin - the day before, childless women make a pilgrimage to Tsambika Monastery to pray for fertility.
28 October: National Day.
14 November: Feast of the Patron Saint of Rhodes, Konstantinos Idertos, when priests from all over the Dodecanese gather at Rhodes.

Faliraki: One of the island's most popular resorts, location of many large hotels, and only 15 km from Rhodes Town. The long beach has full sports facilities, especially water-skiing. It is possible to visit the island's biggest ceramics factory, Neofitou, which produces up to 1200 pieces a day. See **BEACHES 1, EXCURSION 3.**

Feraclos Castle: Near the village of Haraki. The ruins of one of the most powerful medieval fortresses built by the Knights and used as a prison for both war and civil prisoners. To the north are the remains of ancient tombs and a church, Aghia Agatha, which is decorated with 15th and 17thC frescoes. See **EXCURSION 3, WHAT TO SEE 2.**

Filerimos: 13 km from Rhodes Town on the west coast road.
The site of the Doric city of Ialyssos, one of the three ancient cities of
Rhodes. The acropolis dominates the area and shows why it was such a
strategic position. From the Classical period one can see the Temple of
Athena and Zeus Polieus (4thC BC) built in Doric style on the foun-
dations of a sanctuary probably of Phoenician origin. On the left the
underground chapel of St George boasts some restored mural paintings
of the 14th and 15thC. On the right the Baptismal font of an early
Christian Church marks the way to the restored church of Panagia of
Filerimos - part of a monastery founded by the Knights of St John.
Further up the road are the ruins of the castle of the Knights. Entrance
to site is 200 Drs, part of site closed Mondays. See **EXCURSION 1**.

Food: Popular Greek dishes that are available include: *moussaka -*

minced meat, aubergine, potato and bechamel sauce; *pastitsio* - minced meat in bechamel sauce; *dolmades* - stuffed vine leaves; *keftedes* - spicy meat balls; *souvlaki* - chunks of meat cooked on a spit often served in pitta bread with salad as a sort of Greek fast food; *taramasalata* - fish roe and cream; *tzatziki* - cucumber, yoghurt and garlic; *metzes* - a range of small dishes served to accompany drinks or as a starter. Fish dishes are abundant on Rhodes and can be served in a variety of ways. Fish is priced by weight and tends to be more expensive than meat. See RESTAURANTS, **Eating Out.**

Hairdressers: Hairdressing is relatively inexpensive, ranging from 1000 Drs upwards for a cut. Salons on the island include: *Nikos,* 21 Iroon Politechniou St.; *Morphy,* 7 Alexandra Diakou St. and *Coiffure Pierina,* 6 Amohostou St.

Halki: A mountainous island with few roads which is sparsely inhabited except for two villages. Niborio is the principal village and is sited round the harbour. Although there are no hotels, accommodation is available in private houses. The nearest beach is Pandemos Beach, a ten-minute walk on the other side of the hill behind the town. Chora, 4 km from Niborio, was a flourishing centre in the 18th and 19thC but is now practically deserted. The medieval castle with the ruins of a church behind it offers a magnificent view from its location above the village. Access to Halki is by boat from Kamiros Skala. There are, usually, daily sailings at 1500 but times vary at the discretion of the boat owners. The trip takes 1.5 hr and the price is negotiable with the boatman but is approximately 1800 Drs. Don't forget to check times for return sailings. See **ISLANDS**.

Health: The most common ailments are those caused by over-indulgence of sea, sun or food. Care should be taken with regard to these matters. Particular attention should be paid to avoiding reheated food. One local problem can be the pink and purple jellyfish. If stung rub the wound with ammonia and if problems persist see a doctor. EEC members do have reciprocal health coverage but private holiday insurance is a good idea as the Greek service is not as extensive as in the UK. *Hospital* (with 24 hour out-patient clinic): Evrou Stavrou.Tel: 2555; *English-speaking doctor:* Dr Sotiriou, 85 Amerikas St. Tel: 29333 - emergency number 30455. *English-speaking dentist:* Dr Papazacharias, 32 Polytechniou St. Tel: 24516.

Ialyssos: The most ancient finds on Rhodes are located here and date from 16 BC. It was the point of disembarkation of invading forces and was also the location of country residences for the rich Venetian merchants, the Knights and the Ottoman Turks. See **EXCURSION 3**.

Inns, The: Each of the seven tongues of the order of the Knights of St John had their own residency which was known as an Inn. Five of these Inns were located on the Avenue of the Knights (See **A-Z**). The Inn of France is the best preserved example and it has an interesting facade with an off-centre doorway decorated with various coats of arms. It is still occasionally used as a recital hall. Next to the Inn of France is the Inn of Spain, built in a style that reflects its Catalan influence. The Inn of Italy was restored during the period of the Italian occupation to resemble the original building. The Inn of Provence was a later addition to the Avenue, dating from the early 15thC and containing a less ornate facade than its counterparts. Nothing remains of the Inn of Germany bar a plane tree to mark the site. The Inn of England is situated on Museum Square and was originally built in 1493, but was destroyed in 1851 by an earthquake, rebuilt in 1919 by the Italians and further restored by the British after the Second World War. The Inn of Auvergne is also situated away from the Avenue of the Knights on Simi Square. Today it houses the state offices. See **WALK I.**

Ixia: 3 km south of Rhodes on the west coast this small village has been swamped by a series of hotel complexes dating back to the 1960s.

Jewish Quarter: Located to the south east of the Old Town, near St Catherine's Gate. Plateia Matiron Eyreon means Square of the Martyrs and the tiled fountain topped with three sea horses is dedicated to the Jews transported from Rhodes during the Second World War. The square is also the location of the archbishop's palace (15thC).

Kalimnos: The island's main town is Pothea which contains its colourful houses, an animated market and a local museum with displays of how early 20thC Greeks lived. Sponge fishing is a main industry and the local sponge factory takes in organized visits. North of Pothea is the cave of the Seven Virgins with various inscriptions and votive alcoves. The beautiful beach at Vathy, 6 km north of Pothea on the east coast, is served by a regular bus service. See **ISLANDS.**

Kalithea: The mineral springs and thermal waters here have been known for their healing properties since ancient times. Hippocrates recommended them for kidney disorders, rheumatism and arthritis. The thermal baths were added by the Italians in 1929 but today lie abandoned. A series of arches encircle a spring in the hollow of the bay and, further up the rocks, are the baths paved in black and white pebbles. There is also a small pleasant beach. The site retains a certain charm and is located 10 km from Rhodes Town. See **BEACHES 1, EXCURSION 3, WHAT TO SEE 2 .**

Kamiros, Ancient: Situated 34 km from Rhodes on the west coast road. One of the three ancient cities of Rhodes and the only one built without fortifications. It is an extensively excavated site and the ruins give an excellent idea of the layout of the original city. The ruins include the Agora with its Doric stoa from the 3rdC BC, an aqueduct and the temple of Kamira Athena next to which stands the Panghia monastery. See **WHAT TO SEE 2.**

Kamiros Skala: 48 km from Rhodes Town. A small quay for fishing boats and cargoes from Halki. There are also three tavernas and this is a regular coach stop.

Karpathos: Pigadia is the main port and located nearby are the remains of an ancient city. The island has few tourist facilities. Arkassa lies 10 km south west of Pigadia and has a good beach and the remains of a Byzantine church. There are charming villages throughout the island but these would have to be visited on foot as there are practically no roads. See **ISLANDS.**

Kasos: Fry is the small capital town and contains an art museum and the monastery of Aghios Mamas. Within walking distance are two intriguing caves - Ellino Kamares which is partially concealed by a Hellenistic wall and Selia which is more natural with stalagmites and stalactites. There are bus links to various picturesque beaches and towns around the island. See **ISLANDS**.

Kastellorizo: 95 km from Rhodes, and close to the Turkish coast but with a distinct Greek flavour. Accommodation is cheap, delicious seafood is available and there is a tiny but interesting museum located in an old mosque. There are also the remains of a Knight's castle. Parasta cavern is a worthwhile excursion. Free sailings from Mandraki as the Greek government is trying to develop tourism on the island.

Knights: The Knights of St John of Jerusalem (or Knights of Rhodes and later Malta). They were formed in the 11thC as a charitable brotherhood to take care of the poor and the sick in the hospital of Jerusalem, built by the merchants of Amalfi. They soon became a mili-

tary order, sworn to defend the Holy Sepulchre and fight the Moslems. They became the rivals of the Knights Templar and were obliged to retire to Cyprus and from there to Rhodes which they took by force after a two year siege.

The order consisted of knights, chaplains and serving brothers who followed the knights into action. They were later divided into seven sections representing the seven languages or 'tongues' each of which had a bailiff. The Council of Bailiffs was presided over by the Grand Master elected for life by the Knights. For two centuries they fought the invading Turks successfully but were finally obliged to surrender the island in 1522 after a long siege. The Grand Master and 180 survivors left for Crete and from there went to Malta in 1530.

Kos: Considered the second major island of the Dodecanese group. Kos Town is of diverse historical interest with Archaic, Classical, Hellenistic and Roman remains. The most striking are the Castle of the Knights of St John which was built during the 15th and 16thC using materials from the ruins of an ancient acropolis on same site. (0900-1530 Mon., Wed.-Sat., 0930-1430 Sun. 100 Drs.)

Kos town hall features a turreted clock tower and mosaic entrance and is a magnificent example of Italian architecture. It is now an administrative building for the police and courts. Also to be seen is the Casa Romana a 3rdC house which has remarkable mosaic floors and frescoes. There are numerous pools, rooms and courtyards with ruins of a once impressive Hellenistic mansion in the gardens. (0900-1500 Mon.-Sat., 0930-1430 Sun. 100 Drs.) Hippocrates was born on Kos and the Archaeological Museum contains a famous statue of him which was found at Odeon of Kos. The Ancient Sanctuary at Asclepion was the site of Hippocrates' 5thC BC medical school; the first in the world. Built on five levels on a hill behind the town it includes Roman Baths, the elegant Temple of Apollo and Minor and Major Temples of Asclepion. The archaeological site near the waterfront at Agora contains a temple of Aphrodite, a Temple of Hercules and a Roman basilica.

Beaches around Kos tend to be extremely crowded. Continue round to Lampi on the northern tip of the island for a quiet beach. Thermi, with its black sand and pebbles, is a good beach with hot springs which make the sea warm. The best beach on the island is 5 km east of Kamani in the south.

Kos can be visited in one day but merits a longer stay. All types of accommodation are available. See **ISLANDS**

Kremasti: Some of the most beautiful examples of Geometric and Archaic vases that can be seen in the Archaeological Museum were found in the the necropoles around Kremasti. Of interest in the town itself is the small church leaning against the ruins of a medieval castle. In the village is a large modern church decorated in the Byzantine style which was paid for by villagers who had emigrated to the USA. See **EXCURSION 1**.

Laerma: The village closest to the geographical centre of the island. Approached from Lindos and the east coast via a picturesque drive through woodland (some unfortunately destroyed in fires). 4 km south west of the village is the 9thC monastery of Moni Thari (See **CHURCHES**) nestling in the hollow of the valley. The monastery has a 13thC Byzantine church with cupola and original wall paintings covered over in parts by paintings of 16th and 17thC. The church's beautiful icons include one of St Michael, to whom the monastery is dedicated.

Laundry: Hotel staff can normally arrange contact with the numerous dry cleaners located in the New Town. There is a launderette (cost 200 Drs) called *Lavomatic* situated at 32, 28th Octovriou Street.

Leros: The main town of Platanaos is built on the side of a hill crowned with a Byzantine fortress which was restored by the Knights of St John. A road leads from Platanos to the port of Lakki. The best beaches on the island are the clean, sandy and usually deserted beaches at Gourna and Vromolithois. There is a good taxi service on the island, some buses, but cycling can be the best means of transport. See **ISLANDS**.

Lindos: 56 km from Rhodes Town on the east coast road. The second town of Rhodes Island and one of the three ancient cities. This beautiful

town is dominated by a steep hill crowned with the Acropolis of Lindos. The town itself is grouped around two small bays serving as harbours. There are some medieval houses, many with Arab influences, but most houses date from the 16thC. The streets are paved with black pebbles in traditional motifs and some passages are decorated with mosaics. The doorways, intricately carved and painted, add to the charm of the town. The ancient Acropolis is enclosed by walls within which are the 13 restored colums of the Doric Stoa (200 BC) which stand in front of the stairs leading up the 4thC BC Lindian Athena. This beautiful setting has a superb view and the walk up is not too strenuous if taken at a gentle pace. Donkey rides are available part of the way (0800-1700 daily , 0900-1700 Sun.).

Further sites of interest include the Crusader Fortress on the rock that stands 125 m above town. The Church of the Assumption of the Madonna, which was rebuilt in 1489 and houses colourful 18thC frescoes, lies between the town and the Acropolis. In addition to the sights of antiquity, Lindos also has some of the finest stretches of beaches on the island. The town can become very crowded with visitors in the high season. See **BEACHES, EXCURSION 3, LINDOS, WHAT TO SEE 2.**

Mandraki Harbour: Now serves as a pleasure boat harbour. Two columns bearing bronze deer, the emblem of Rhodes, stand over the harbour where the Colossus of Rhodes was reputed to have stood. Along the mole protecting the west side of the harbour are three wind-mills which used to provide flour for the cargo ships. The 1446 fortress of St Nicholas still guards the end of the pier but is no longer in use.

Money: Travellers cheques are widely accepted in shops and res-taurants but at lower exchange rates than at banks. Passport identifica-tion is required when cashing cheques. Travellers cheques can also be exchanged at the Post Office. Major international credit cards are also widely accepted. In case of loss of money contact the police and take your passport with you. The police will give you a form to forward to your insurance company.

Moni Skiadi: Near the village of Messanagros above Apolakkia Bay in the south west of the island. This monastery was founded in the Byzantine era and restored in the 18thC. Although now somewhat dilapidated the church contains several interesting frescoes. See CHURCHES.

Monolithos: Situated a short distance south west of the village of Monolithos (80 km from Rhodes Town) is Monolithos Castle perched on top of a 230 m high rock. Access is easily gained to the castle via a flight of stone steps. From here the Knights used to keep watch over the sea. Although now in ruins there is a small white-washed chapel, still used, inside the ruins. There are incredible views over the sea and surrounding countryside and you can still see the old walls surrounding the rocky plateau of the summit. See **WHAT TO SEE 2**.

Mosque of Suleiman: Erected in honour of Suleiman the Magnificent's conquest of the Knights in 1522 and built on the site of the Church of the Apostles. This is the largest mosque in Rhodes and contains a stone minaret, red plaster walls and a bright airy interior. See **CHURCHES, WALK 1**.

Mount Ataviros: This is the highest mountain on the island with a peak of 1215 m. At the summit are the ruins of a sanctuary dedicated to Zeus and also the small church of St John the Evangelist. The views from the summit are superb. On the lower eastern slopes towards Aghios Isidoros are the remains of a monastery, Ag. Iannis Artamitis, which held an important position between the 12th and 14thC. See **EXCURSION 4**.

Museum of Decorative Arts: Housed in what used to be the arsenal, it contains traditional Dodecanese costumes, furniture, ceramic plates from Lindos and carved sea chests. On the right of the entrance door are a pile of cannonballs stacked ready for use during the siege of of 1522. See **WHAT TO SEE 1**.

New Market: Situated in the New Town close to Mandraki Harbour, this impressive polygonal building encloses a courtyard area with food stalls and small shops. On the west side are meat stalls and butcher shops. The fish market is in the domed building in the centre. There are also several cafés and bars in the market.

Newspapers: Foreign papers and magazines appear the day after publication and are mainly to be found in the bookshops opposite the post office, around the Mandraki area and in larger hotels.

Nightlife: Most of the discos, bars and night clubs are to be found in the New Town of Rhodes in the Academias area. Outwith Rhodes a lively nightscene can be found in such towns as Ixia, Lindos and Faliraki. Prices are fixed by law according to the class of establishment. Latest closing time is 0230. See **NIGHTLIFE.**

Nisyros: Mandraki is both a charming village and the main port on this island. It lies beneath the monastery of Panagia Spiliana which contains a small 10thC chapel of Holy Mary. The Castle was built by the Knights. However, the island's main attraction is the volcano crater with its hot sulphur vents. In Loutra there is a spa of sulphurous spring water. Situated close to the crater is the picturesque village of Nikia. An interesting view of the surrounding area is possible from Agios Theodori. See **ISLANDS.**

Opening Times: *Shops:* 0800-1430 Mon., Wed., Sat.; 0800-1330 Tues.; 1700-2100 Thur. and Fri.
Banks: 0800-1400 Mon.-Fri. (some open in the afternoon). Summer hours: 0800-1300, 1700-2100 Mon.-Fri.; 0800-1300 Sat.
Museums and Sites: 0900-1330, 1600-1800. 1000-1630 Sundays and bank holidays.
Nightclubs: All close at 0230 at the latest.
Restaurants: Lunchtime 1100-1500; dinner 1800 till very late, usually stop serving at midnight.

Orientation: Rhodes Town is situated on the northern tip of the island. From this point there are two possible routes down the island: the east coast road with popular resorts taking you down through Lindos to Katavia in the south, or the west coast road, less busy once past the built-up resorts of Trianda Bay, taking you down to Apolakia three quarters of the way down the coast. A good tarred road now almost completely encircles the island, only about 10 km of rough road is left south of Apolakia. The interior of the island is mountainous with isolated villages and woody hills and valleys. The highest mountain is Mount Ataviros which lies halfway down the west coast.

Palace of the Grand Masters: This 300 room castle with moats, drawbridges, watchtowers and battlements dates from the late 14thC. It survived the 1522 siege reasonably well only to be blown up in 1856 by an explosion in an ammunition store. It was rebuilt by the Italians in the early 1900s and used as a seat of Italian government and to enter-tain King Victor-Emmanuel II and Mussolini. Worth visiting for one of the finest collections of Hellenistic and early Byzantine mosaics.

Passports and Customs: There are no visa requirements. A valid passport is required for a stay of up to three months, except for EEC members for whom the period of stay is unlimited. There is no limit on the sum of money brought into the country in foreign exchange but if it exceeds $500 it should be declared. It is illegal to export more money than is imported. If money is received from abroad whilst in Greece proof of the bank transaction must be produced.

There are no vaccination requirements if you come from an epidemic-free country.
There are some restrictions on package tourists visiting Turkey from Rhodes and one might have problems getting back into Greece afterwards. Enquire at customs before travelling.

Patmos: The island is most associated with St John as it was here that the Book of Revelations was written in AD 95. The Monastery of the Apocalypse, situated 2 km south of Skals, is on the actual spot where the book was supposed to have been written. The main monastery dedicated to the saint is that of St John the Divine and hundreds of pilgrims come from all over Europe to worship here at Easter. See **ISLANDS.**

Petaloudes: One of the most famous spots on Rhodes.
From mid-June to September the valley is inundated by thousands of small, brightly coloured butterflies (*Callimorpha quadrippunctaria*), probably originating in Turkey. One explanation for this concentration is that the butterflies are attracted by the strong scent of benzoin; a resin produced by one of the variety of trees in the valley. The area is a very popular tourist attraction in the high season. Entry to the Valley of the Butterflies in June-Sept. is 100 Drs, gate open 0830-1700, free the rest of the year. The walk is through a scenic valley with well-constructed paths and bridges, and benches at the main viewing points. There is a small shop for souvenirs and postcards and a taverna 350 m down from the car park.

Pets: Although small domestic pets are allowed onto the island they are not usually accepted at hotels and restaurants. A certificate is required declaring that the animal has been disease free and has had an anti-rabies vaccination within the last 12 months. Veterinary surgeon: Mr Mihali Apostolidis, Koskinou St., Rhodes.

Police: There are two branches of the police force; the general police and the Tourist Police. The main police have green uniforms and deal with normal, civilian problems whilst the Tourist Police have dark grey uniforms and deal specifically with assisting in tourist related problems.

They wear badges indicating what languages they speak. Police head-quarters are near the main post office on Platia Eleftherias.

Post Office: The main post office is located on Platia Eleftheria at Mandraki Harbour. Open daily 0800-2000 in summer (closes one hour earlier in winter). A letter to an EEC destination takes an 80 Drs stamp and a postcard a 60 Drs stamp. A *poste restante* service is available, have your mail addressed to you at; Post Restante, Rhodes, Greece. There is a post office in the Old Town on Orfeos St., 0800-2000, Mon.-Fri.; 0900-1800, Sat.-Sun.

Prassonisi, Cape: 91 km south of Rhodes Town. This is the most southerly point on the island. A path has to be followed for 2 km from the main road over the sandy causeway to reach the rugged windswept point with its view of the lighthouse. See **EXCURSION 4**.

Prophitas Ilias: Third highest mountain on the island with a peak of 780 m. Clad in a beautiful forest of pine, cypress and old cedar trees. There are some marked walks leading up the mountain which pass two Italian-built Alpine-style hotels and a monastery. There is a military installation at the summit. See **EXCURSION 2**.

Public Holidays: 1 and 6 Jan.; 7 and 25 Mar.; first day of Lent; Good Friday; Easter Monday; 1 May; 15 Aug.; 28 Oct.; 14 Nov.; 25 and 26 Dec. See **Events.**

Radio and Television: The radio has news in English, French, German and Arabic between 0730 and 0755.
There are nine TV channels including two Greek, one Turkish, one German, one French, one English/American and one continuous news.

Restaurants: There are all types of restaurants catering for all types of tastes. In tavernas (usually family-run, more informal and cheaper, though not always, than restaurants), you can still go into the kitchen and point at what you want. Greeks eat late and stay up drinking and dancing till the early hours of the morning. Fish, whilst abundant, is

more expensive than meat. The bill always shows two prices, with and without service, and you automatically pay the higher one. Desserts are not traditionally Greek (though many restaurants serve them to cater for tourists) - retire to a coffee house or 'zacharoplasteion' for something sweet after a meal. Many around Rhodes are open all day and till late at night. See **RESTAURANTS**.

Rhodes New Town (Nea Chora): To the north west of the Old Town and surrounding the harbour. First developed in the 16thC during the Turkish occupation when Greeks were forbidden to live in the walled town so they developed settlements outside its walls. Most of the present-day buildings date from the Italian occupation. The New Town contains few buildings of historical interest but is the administrative area with the post office, Town Hall and the Bank of Greece building. The most outstanding structure is the Governor's Palace, resembling the Doge's Palace in Venice and looking strangely out of place here. See **WALK 3**.

Rhodes (Old Town): At the end of the 5thC BC the three ancient cities of the island of Rhodes united to form a fourth; Rhodes on the northern tip of the island. Rhodes Town flourished as a centre of Hellenistic culture. It has also experienced life under Roman, Byzantine, Italian, Crusader, and Ottoman Turk rule. The major architectural influence is from the period of the Knights of St John (1309-1522). It was they who built the Palace of the Grand Masters (see **A-Z**) and enclosed the city (now known as the Old Town) with walls, gates and moats (See **Walls**). In 1522 the Turks took Rhodes and converted many of the churches into mosques. See **WALK 1, 2**.

Rodini Park: Situated only 3 km from Rhodes Town, this forested park is situated on the slopes of a limestone plateau. Within the park is a 3rdC BC necropolis, with Doric columns, traditionally called Tomb of the Ptolemies. It is also thought to have been the site of the Rhodes School of Rhetoric where many famous figures in Greek and Roman history (including Julius Caesar) studied. Today it is a pleasant area for a walk with attractions such as an orchestra playing (in the summer),

bouzouki and international music and an enclosure with Rhodian deer.
See **EXCURSION 1**.

Simi: The island used to be prosperous through sponge fishing and
ship building. It was here that the allied takeover agreement was signed
after the Second World War. Ghialos, the main port on northern side of
island, was declared a historical site in 1971. White houses surround
the bay and many are designed in a Neoclassical style but actually date
from 19thC. Choro is the fortified area on the hill behind Ghialos and
its houses were incorporated within its walls to protect them from
marauding pirates. One has to climb up some 500 steps to reach it
from the harbour. Panorimitis is the site of a magnificent 18thC monastery dedicated to St Michael and is accessible by boat. When a boat
enters the bay the bells of the 12th C church ring. See **ISLANDS**.

Smoking: Cigarettes are sold in kiosks. The kiosk in Mandraki harbour is open late at night. All brands of cigarettes are available and cost
from 170 - 260 Drs. Greek brands are cheaper. Smoking is not allowed
in public places, on local and excursion buses and in most taxis.

Taxis: All taxis are privately owned but there is a new office operating radio taxis. Tel: 29861. Minimum charge is 130 Drs. Tips are not obligatory but customary. The main taxi rank in Rhodes Town is in Platia Alexandrias at the south end of Mandraki, adjacent to the New Market.

Telephones and Telegrams: This is a separate service from the post office. Called OTE (Greek Telecommunications Organisation), there is one situated on Amerikis Street and another one near Platia Argirokastro. Open every day from 0600-2300, Apr.-Oct. You can make your calls from here or from a call box. The blue and red phones are for local calls and take 5 Drs coins. The orange ones are for long distance calls and take 5, 10 or 20 Drs coins. Telephone rates are cheaper from 2100-0900 and at weekends. You can send telegrams or make international calls from OTE offices. International calls are metered and you pay the cashier after your call.

Tilos: The main town (which has pleasantly uncrowded beaches) is the port of Livadia. 8 km north of Livadia is Megalochorio whose name means 'big town' but which only contains around 150 inhabitants. The village is dominated by a Venetian Castle. Many tourists come to Tilos for the festival at the Monastery of Aghios Panteleimonos from 25-27 July. See **ISLANDS.**

Time Differences: Two hours ahead of GMT. Clocks in Rhodes are put forward one hour in summer.

Tipping: Considered optional at hotels and restaurants as service is usually included in the bill. 10% is the expected rate for taxis. 20 to 50 Drs for the chambermaid, barber, tour guide, waiter or *mikro* - the small boy who helps out.

Toilets: Most public conveniences are clean and well-maintained and can be found in the New Market, on Alexandrou Papagou, close to the bus terminus; at the Olypic Airways Office at Odhos Ierou Lochou and on Orfeos Street between the Grand Palace Gates and the Clock Tower.

Tourist Information: The NTOG office (National Tourist Organization of Greece) is in the centre of the New Town on Makariou Street, tel: 21921/23635. It is open between 0730 and 1500. The staff are very helpful and most speak either English, French or German. They can offer free leaflets, guidance on choice of hotels, information about rentals and sightseeing information in general.

Transport: Buses are the commonest means of transport. A cheap and regular service operates to all the principal locations in the island (See **Buses**). Mopeds and motorbikes are very popular as they are cheap. However, they can be dangerous especially if used on the less well developed roads on the island (See **Bicycle Hire**). For the tourist, car hire is probably the most comfortable means by which to explore the island (See **Car Hire**).

Trianda: See Ialyssos.

Tsambika Monastery: Close to the summit of Mount Tsambika, this Byzantine cloister dates from the 14thC and consists of five white-

washed cells. From outside the monastery there is a wonderful view over the bay. Each year, on 7 September, childless women make a pilgrimage to this spot. See **EXCURSION 3, CHURCHES**.

Turkish Quarter: The term applies to the area of the Old Town the Turks moved into after their successful conquest of Rhodes in 1522. The Christians resident there at the time were given until sunset to leave the island. The Byzantine churches were converted into mosques by the addition of minarets. The area still has an oriental feel because

of the arched windows and fountains. The Turkish Baths are still in operation.

Walking: Some agencies are beginning to organize walking tours as a means of exploring the more authentic, primitive side of Rhodes. There are routes marked through the countryside by spots of paint on rocks and trees but they are not always to be counted on. Generally speaking you can walk anywhere although there are no large scale maps available. The best months for walking are April, May, June, September and October. Take the usual precautions, wear protection against the sun, carry food and drink and wear good shoes or boots.

Walls, Gates and Moats: In the 15thC the Knights reconstructed and strengthened the already existing walls to better fortify the town against the Turks. Set in the shape of an irregular square the walls are up to 12 m thick in parts. Each section (Tongue) of the Knights was responsible for the defence of a section of the walls. The Turks were later to add thick, round towers called *Koule*. Of the gates in the walls, the three that you are most likely to see, and which are also the most impressive are:

Eleftheria (Liberty or Freedom) Gate: The usual entrance to the Old Town and closest gate to Mandraki. It was reconstructed in the 1920s and named in 1947 to commemorate the unification of Rhodes with Greece. The gate leads into Simi Square. and the ruined Temple of Aphrodite. Adjacent to it, on the seaward side, is the older (15thC) St Paul's gate, a narrow gate leading onto the commercial harbour.

Amboise Gate: The nearest gate to the Palace of the Grand Masters. It is the most spectacular of all the gates, extending across the inner and outer moats. Built in 1512 by Grand Master Aimerie d'Amboise, whose coat of arms is carved on the outer part of the gate.

Marine Gate: This links the eastern part of the Old Town to the Commercial Harbour. It is a grand structure with a high arch with tall, machicolated towers on either side decorated by white marble bas-reliefs of the Virgin Mary, St Peter and St Paul. There is also the coat of arms of Pierre d'Aubusson, the 15thC Grand Master who played a major part in strengthening the town's defences against the Turks.